Craig Armstrong Piano Works

Transcriptions and engraving: Artemis Music Limited
(www.artemismusic.com)

Published 2004

© International Music Publications Limited
Griffin House 161 Hammersmith Road London England W6 8BS

In My Own Words

Music by Craig Armstrong

Heatmiser 2

Words and Music by Craig Armstrong

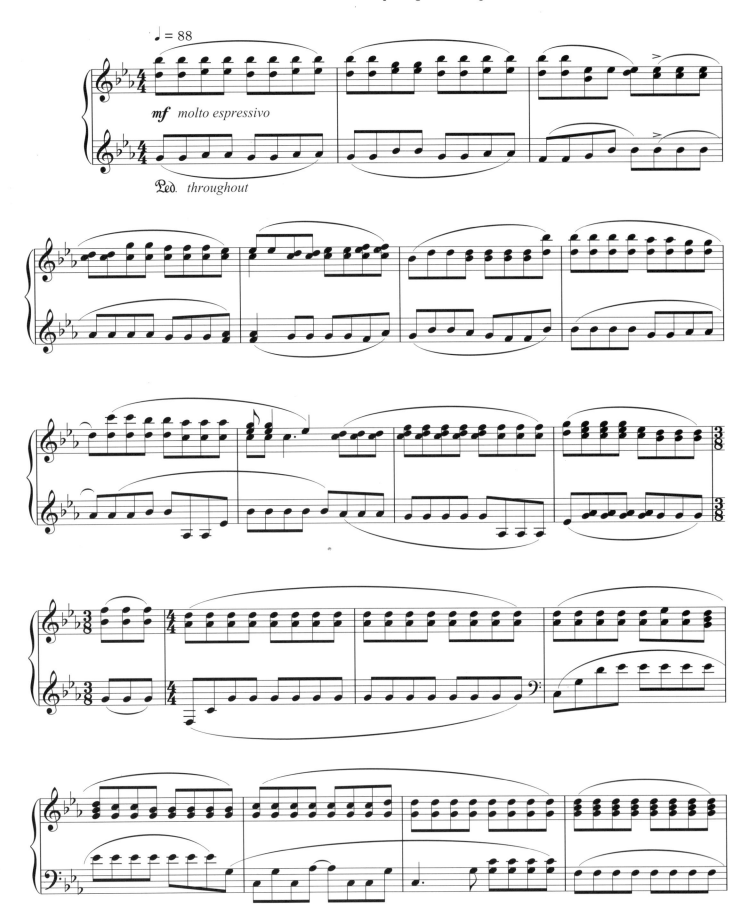

6

Hidden

Music by Craig Armstrong

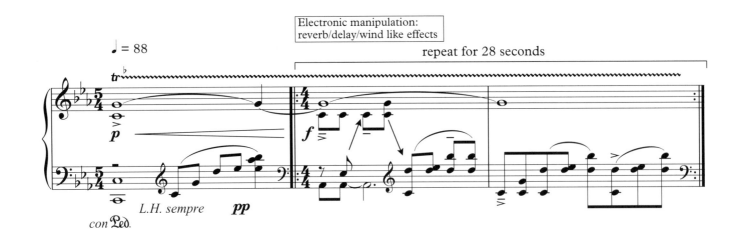

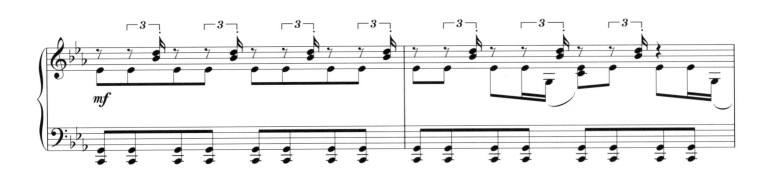

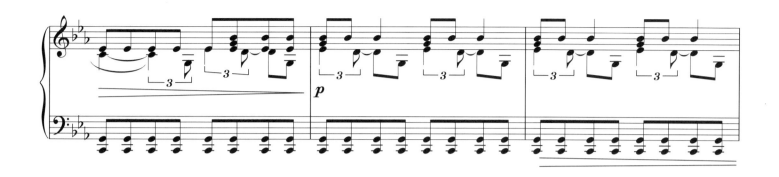

Gentle Piece

Music by Craig Armstrong

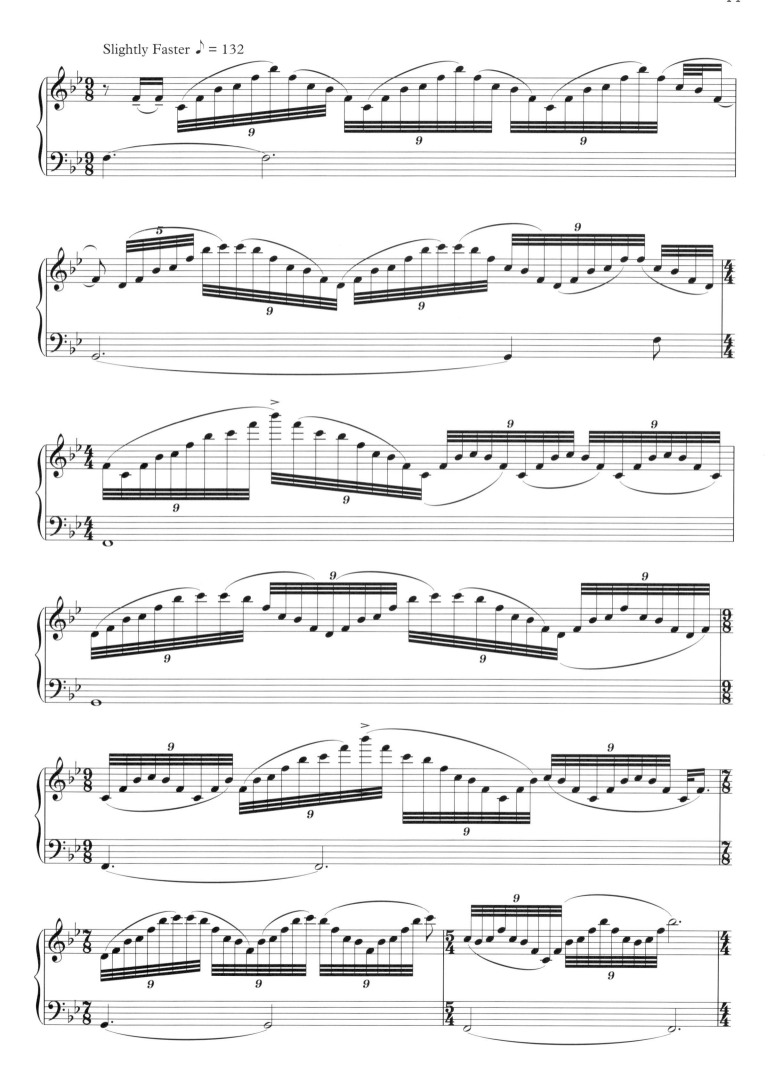

Weather Storm

Words and Music by Craig Armstrong, Robert Del Naja, Andrew Lee Isaac Vowles, Grantley Marshall,
Nellee Hooper, Cedric Napoleon, James Lloyd, Curtis Harmon and Daniel Harmon

Freely, with much rubato ♩ = 88

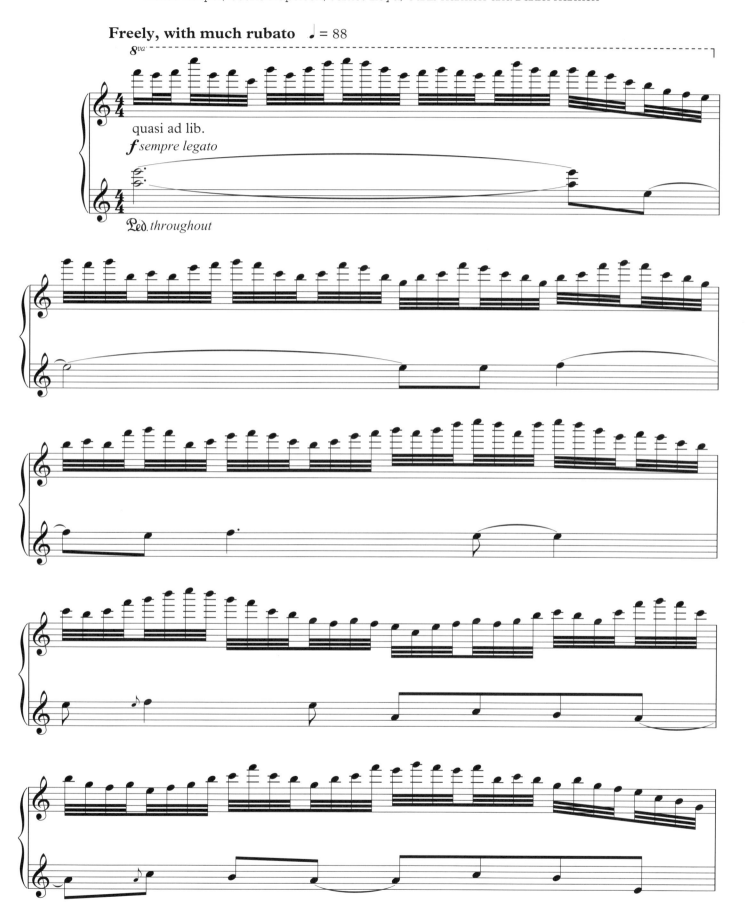

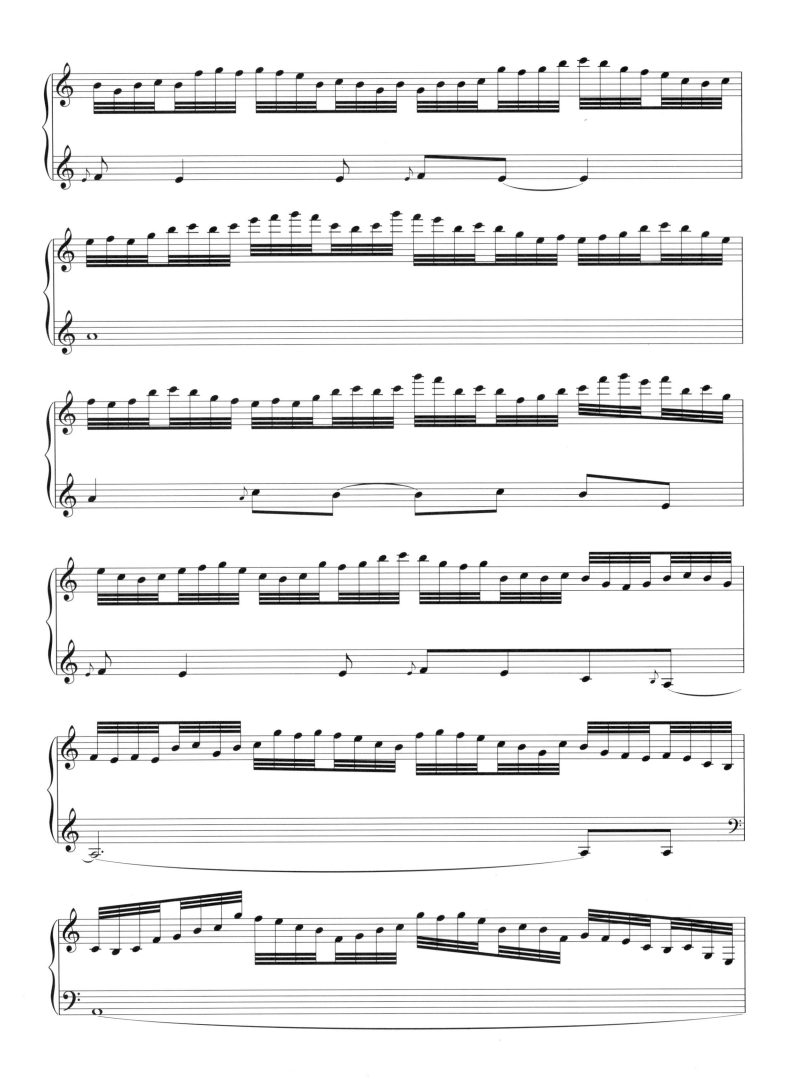

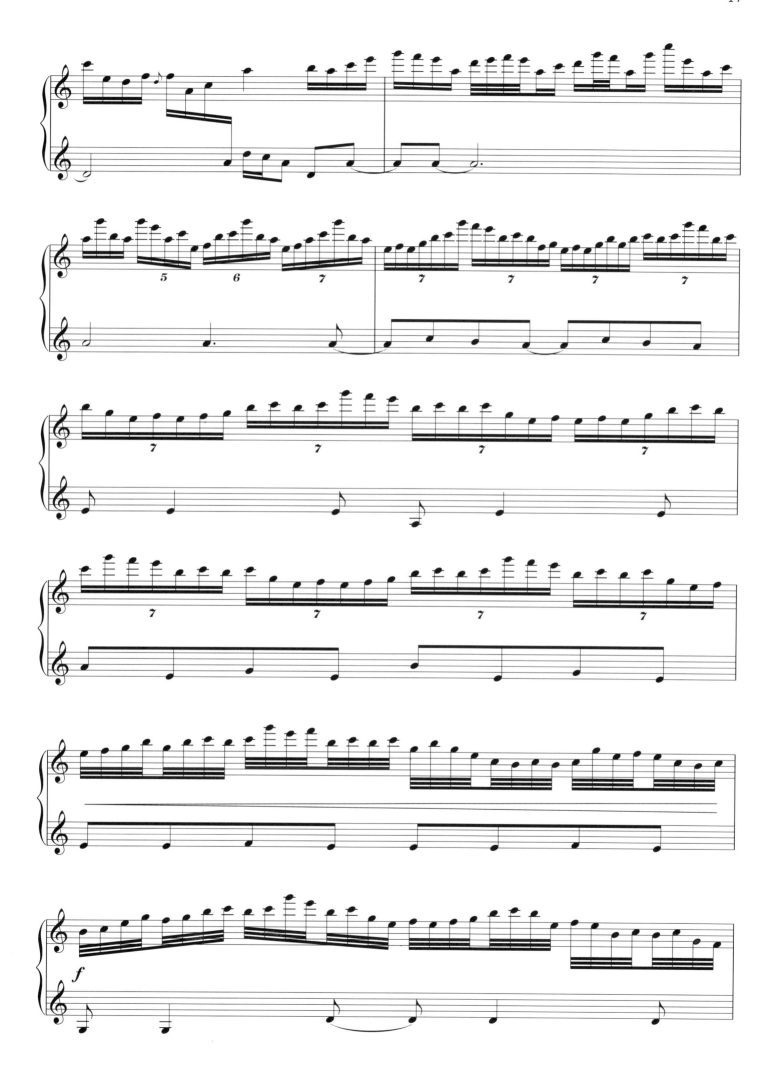

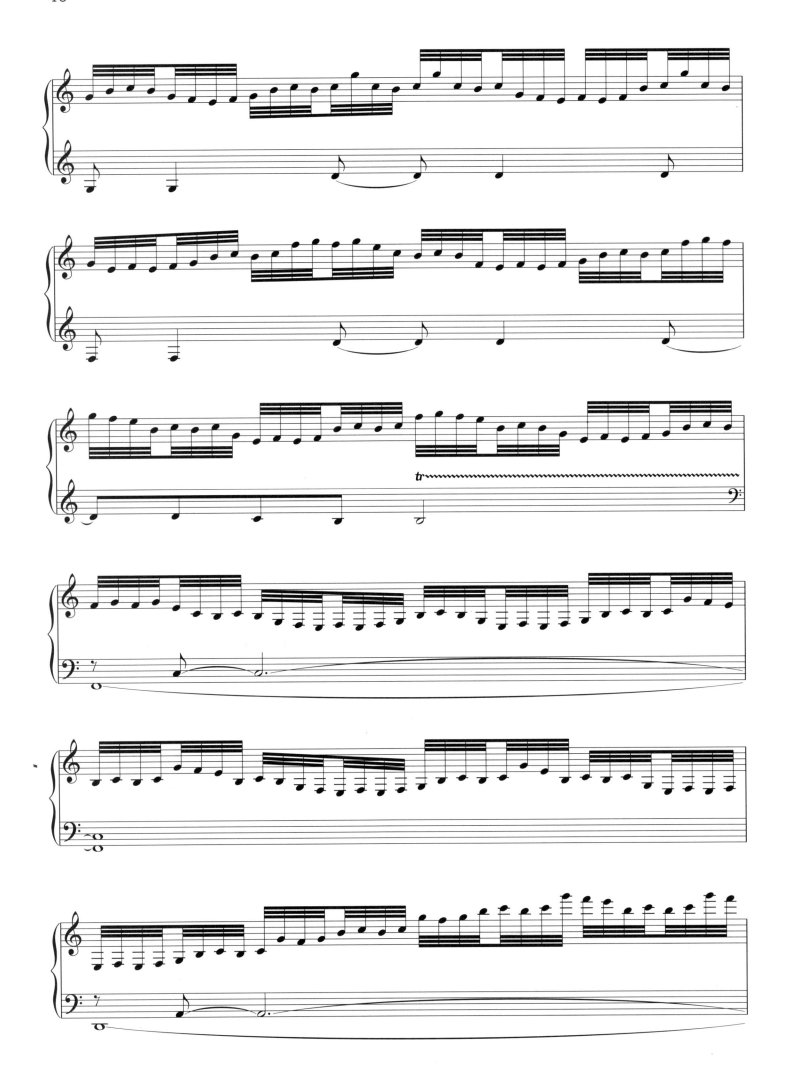

Diffuse

Music by Craig Armstrong

Leaving Paris

Music by Craig Armstrong

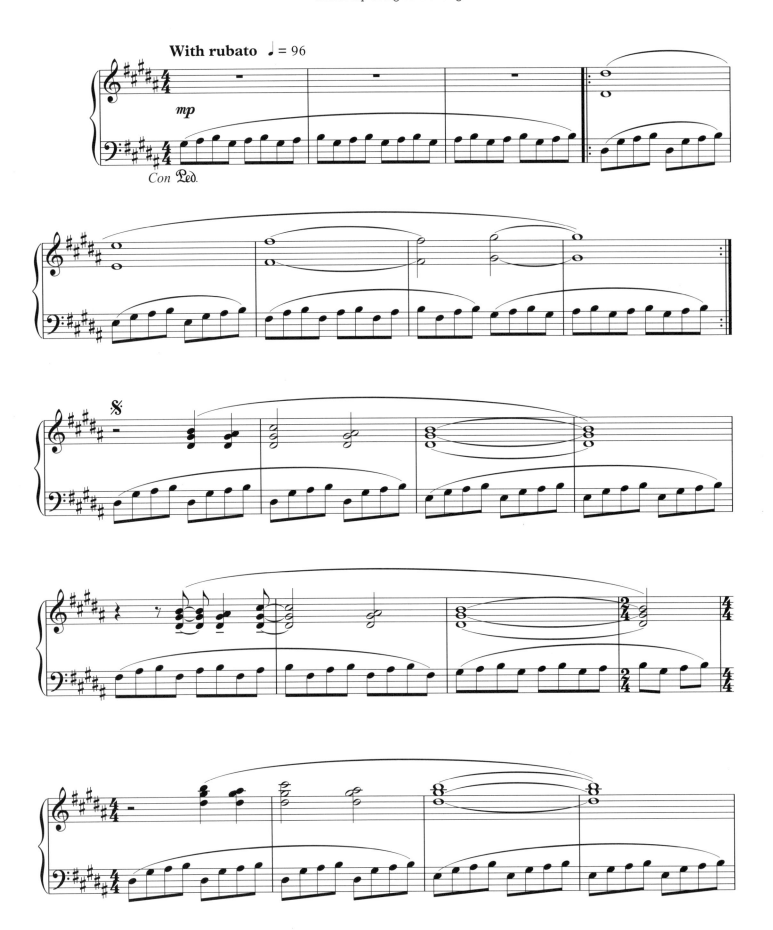

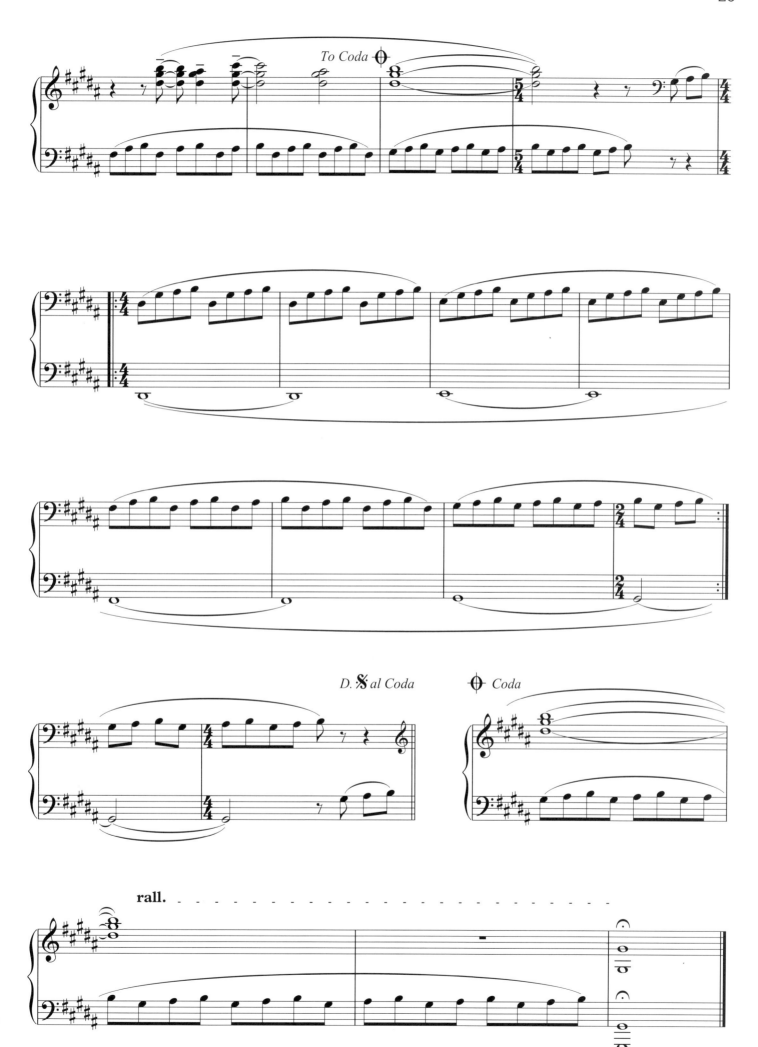

Fugue

Music by Craig Armstrong

Theme from Orphans

Music by Craig Armstrong

1st Waltz

Music by Craig Armstrong

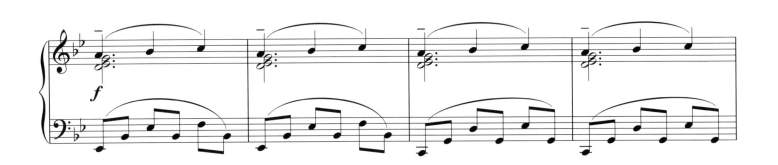

poco rall. _ _ _ _ _ _ _ _ _ _ _ _ _ _ _ _

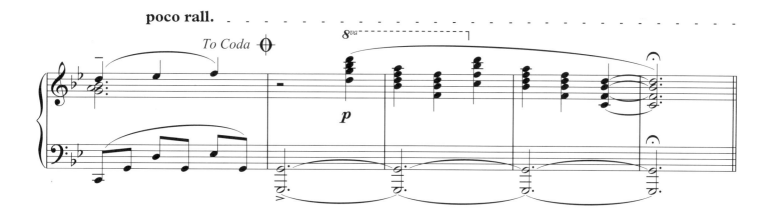

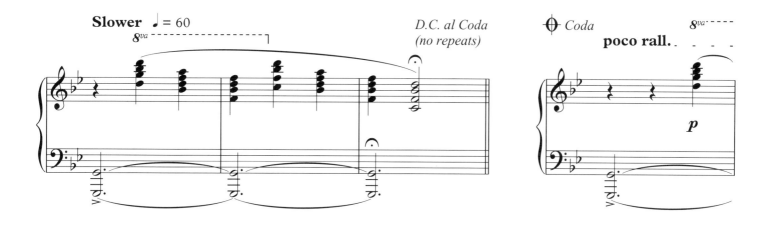

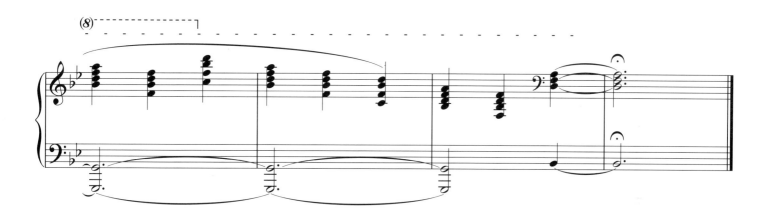

Satine's Theme

Music by Craig Armstrong

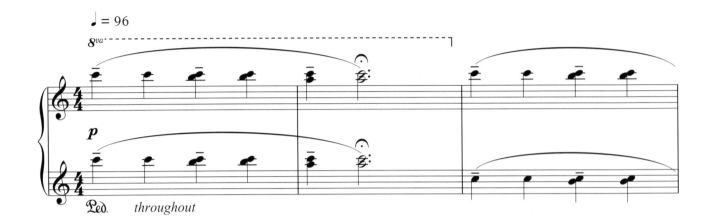

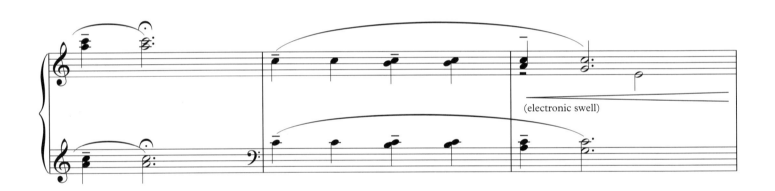

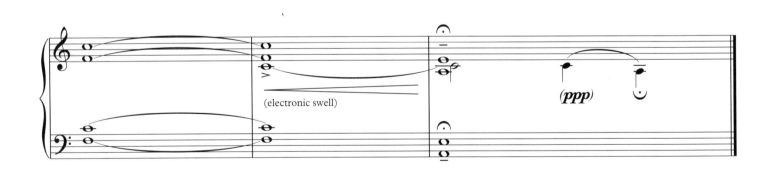

Laura's Theme

Words and Music by Craig Armstrong

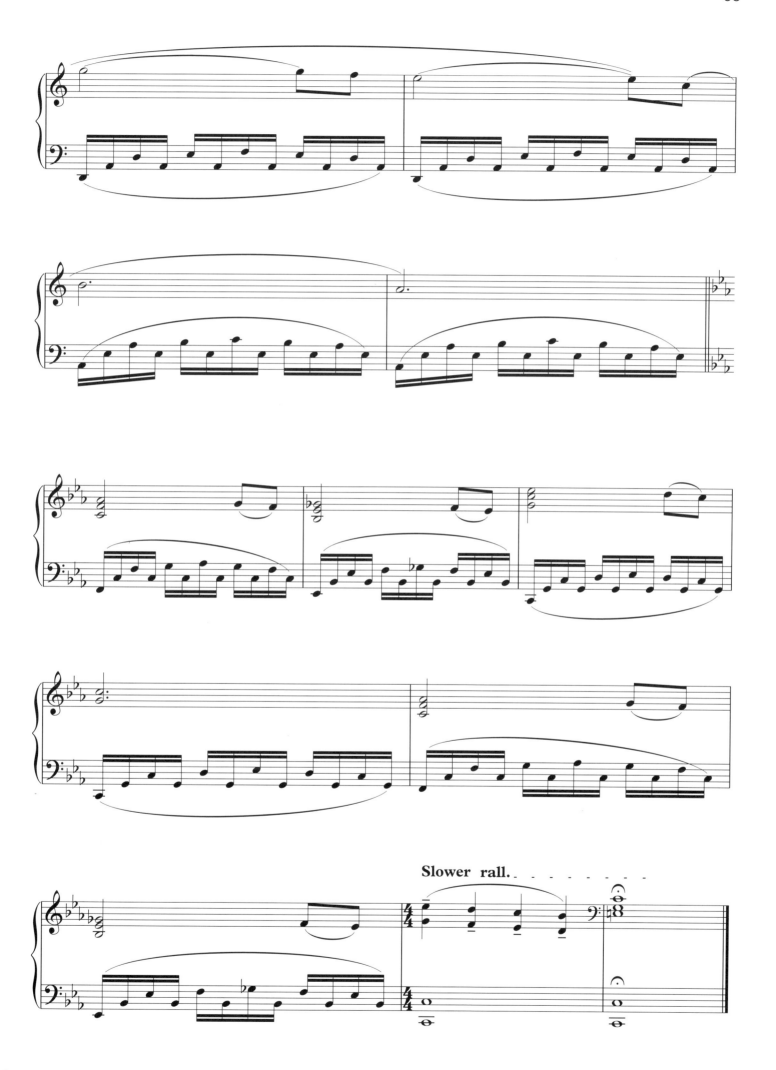

Morning Breaks

Music by Craig Armstrong, Marius De Vries and Paul Andrew Hooper

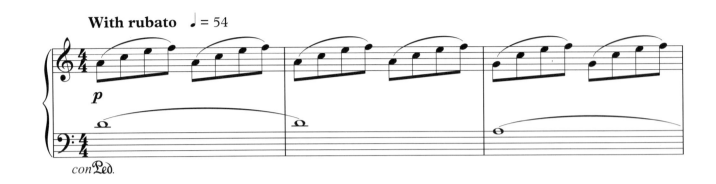

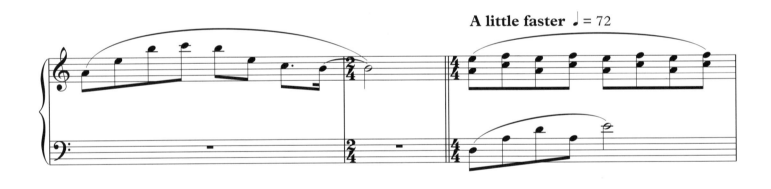

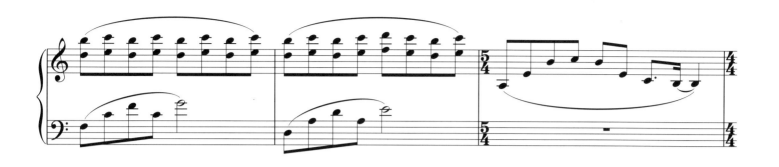

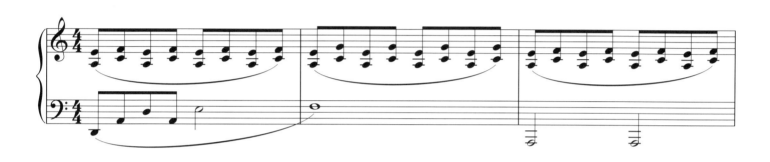

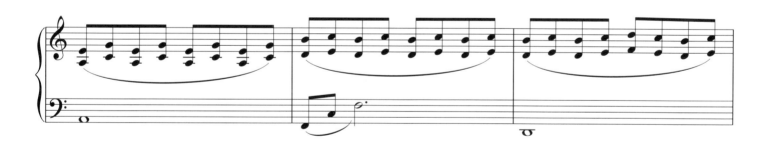

Glasgow Love Theme

Music by Craig Armstrong

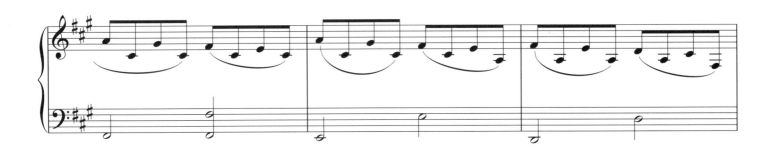

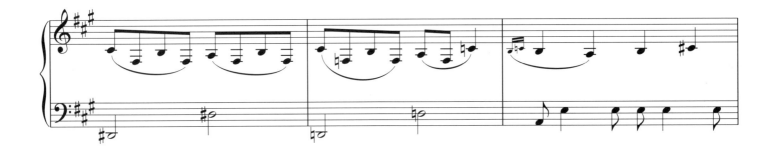

Delay

Music by Craig Armstrong

Hymn 3

Music by Craig Armstrong

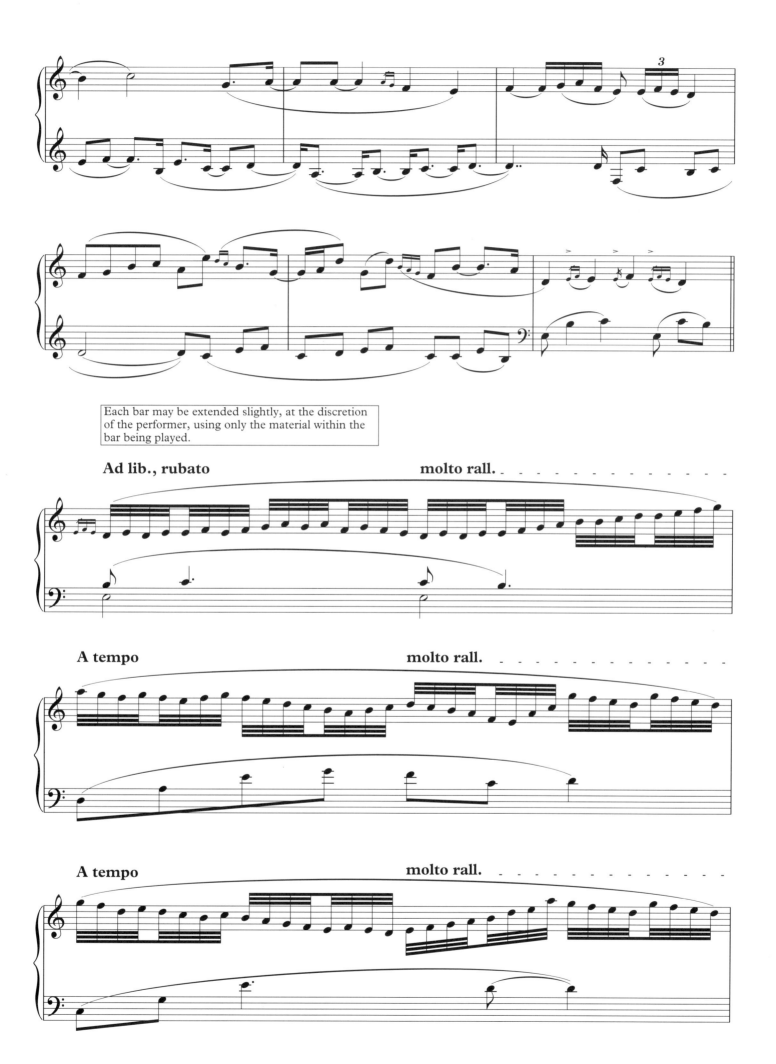

Each bar may be extended slightly, at the discretion of the performer, using only the material within the bar being played.

Ad lib., rubato   molto rall. _ _ _ _ _ _ _ _ _ _ _

A tempo   molto rall. _ _ _ _ _ _ _ _ _ _

A tempo   molto rall. _ _ _ _ _ _ _ _ _ _

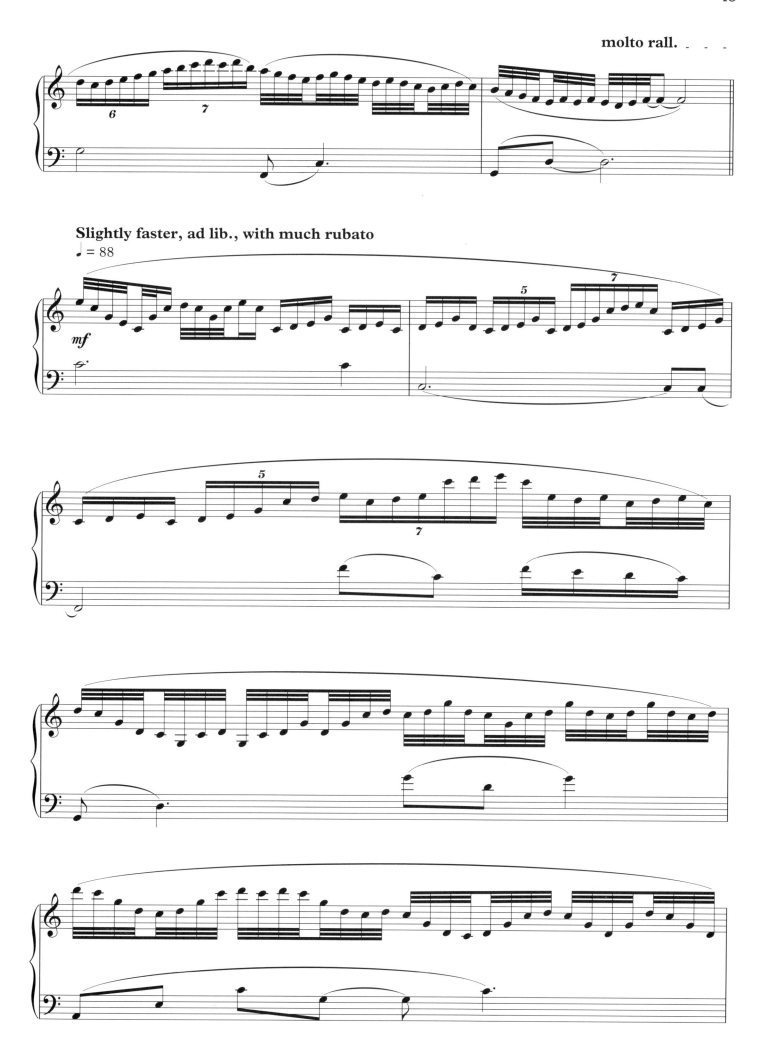

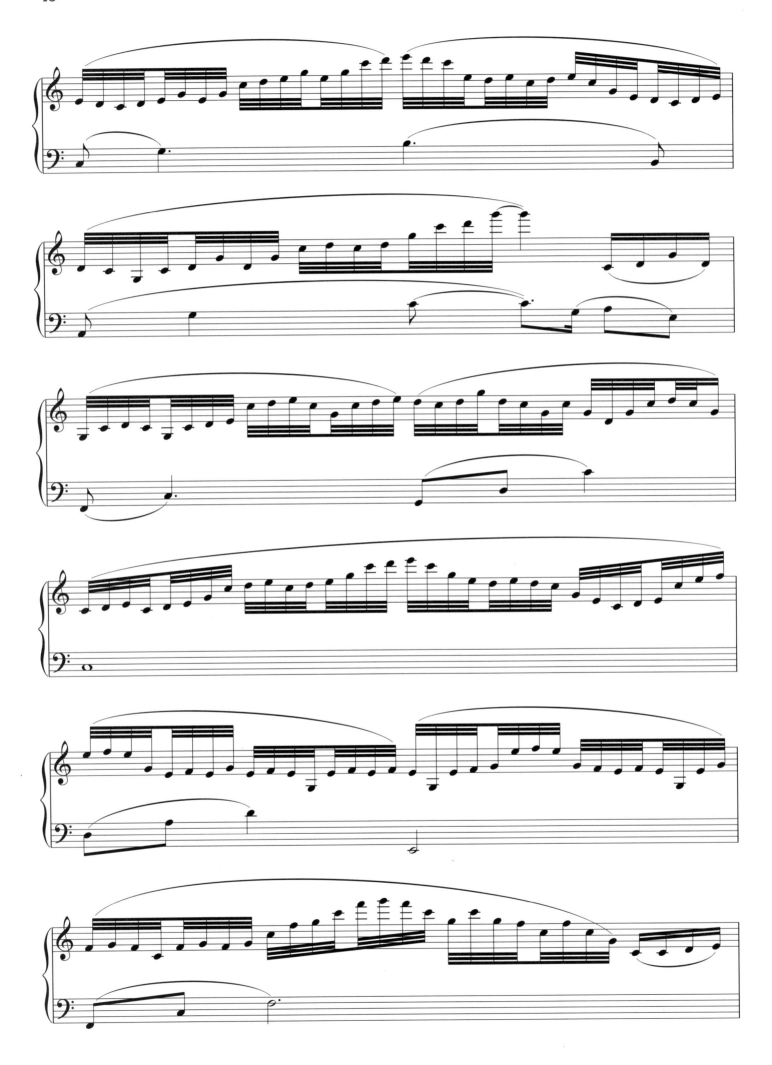

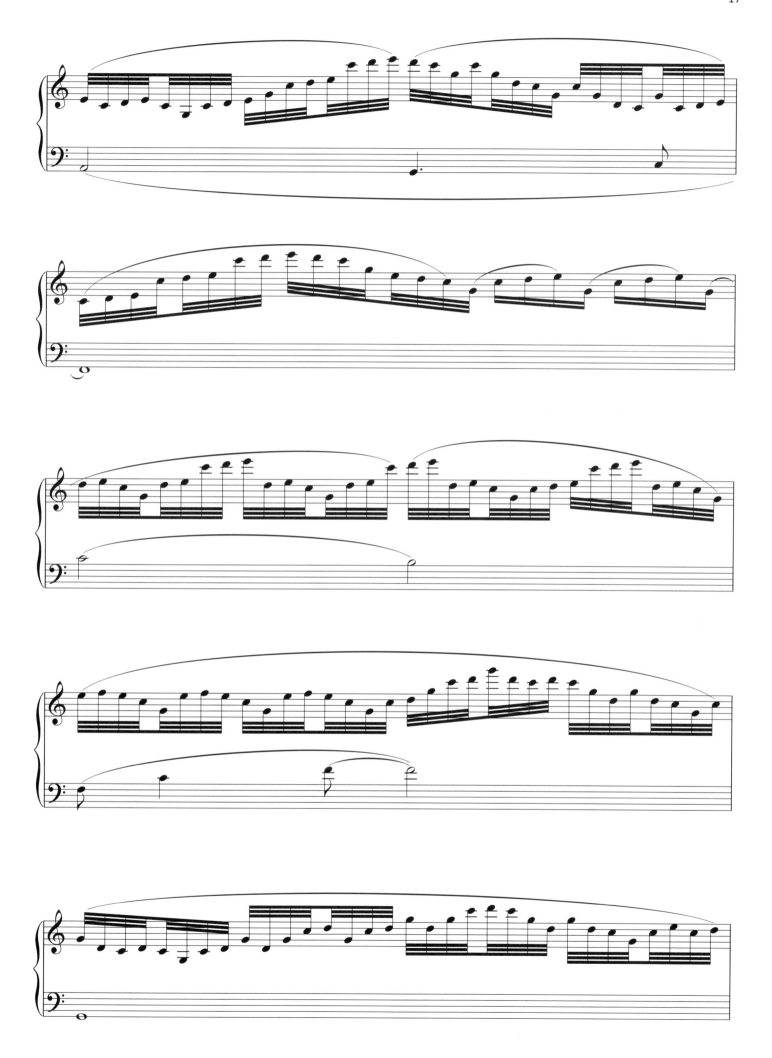

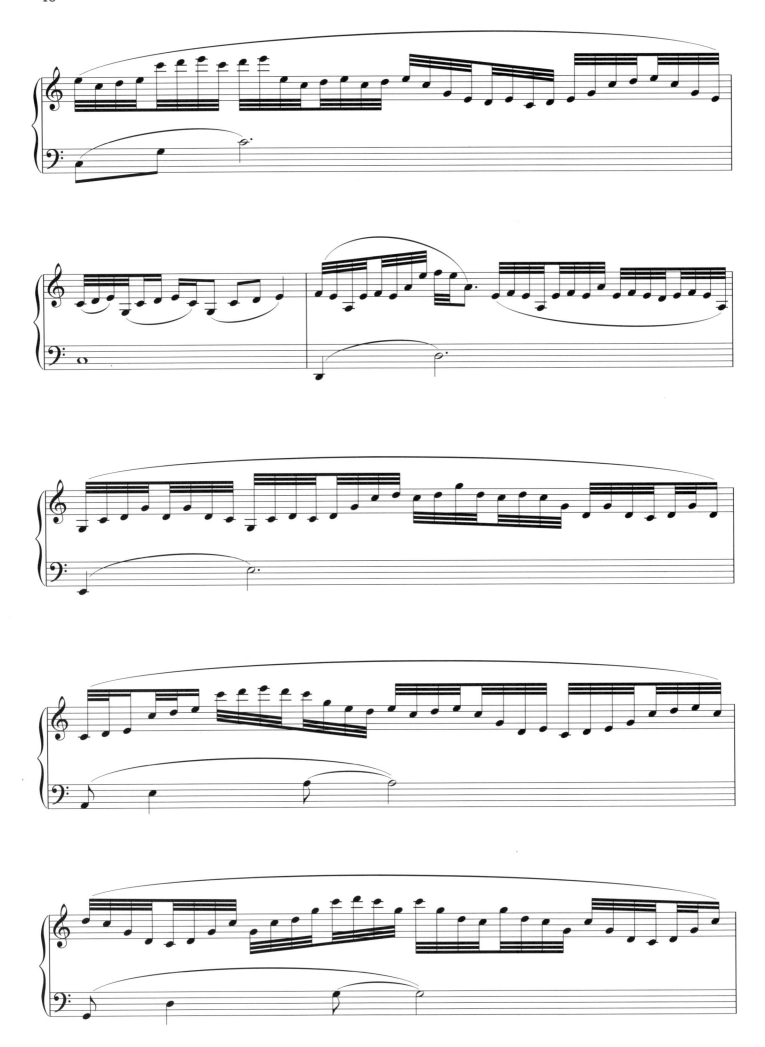

Angelina

Music by Craig Armstrong

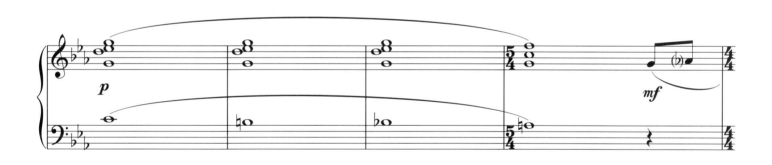

Sunrise

Music by Craig Armstrong

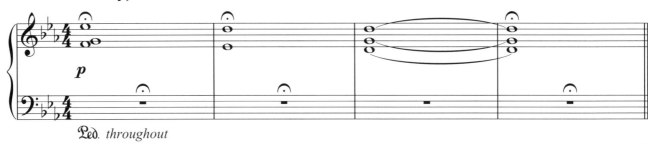

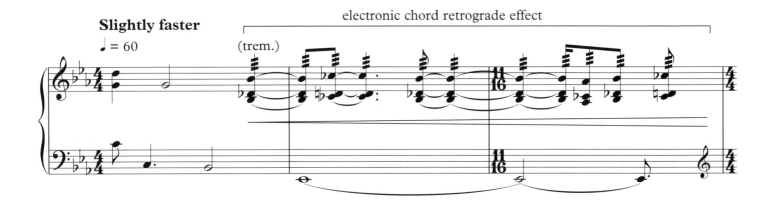

Childhood 2

Music by Craig Armstrong

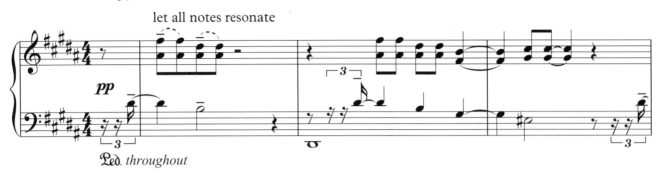

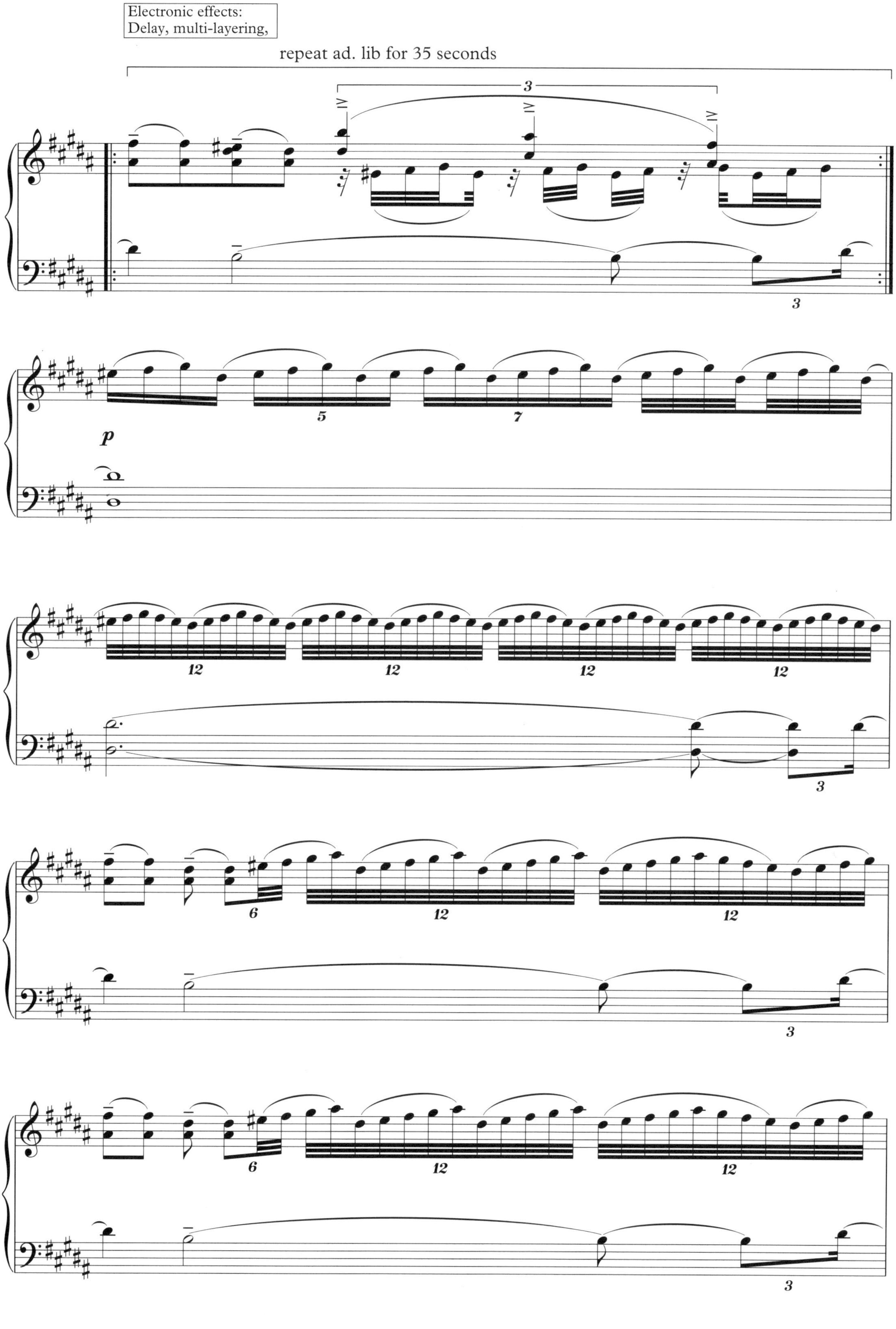
Electronic effects:
Delay, multi-layering,
repeat ad. lib for 35 seconds

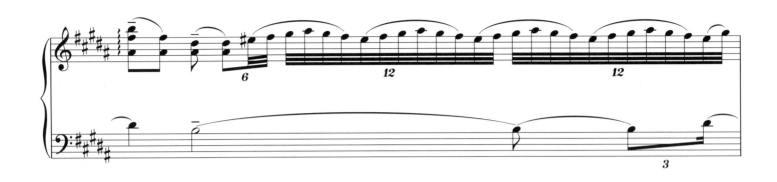

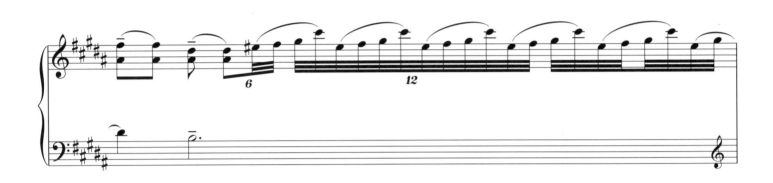

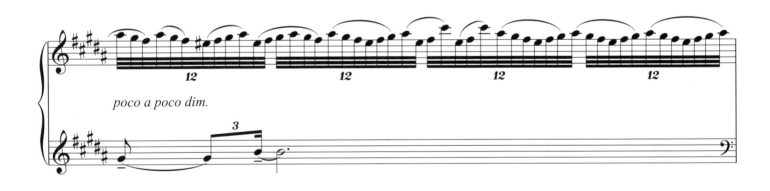

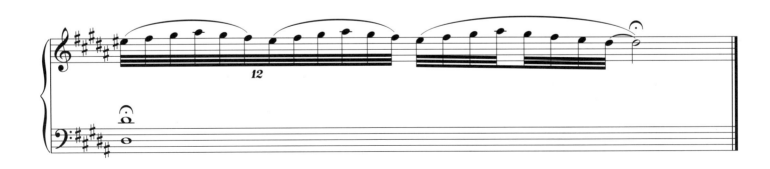